1.

Never finish

This is the first and most important rule of Debrism.

2.

If you do finish something - disown it. Spend years thinking about how much better you could have done it.

3.
If someone says:

"But that was perfect!"

Look into that person's reasons for saying this - think carefully about that person, then dismiss that person's opinion.

4.
Start something new every day.

Do not plan what this thing is.
Just make a vague note on the project, then begin.

5.
Convince yourself that this latest project is 'The New Way'.

Write an impassioned email to yourself explaining why (but resist any further kind of exploration or research).

6.

Write down a snappy or punning title for an unclear thought (e.g. 'Male Art'). Dwell on the title, perhaps consider making it into a book - when this unclear thought refuses to clarify itself, spend hours/months designing a cover for this 'book'.

If a publisher/editor - perhaps in conversation - gets excited about the title of your 'book' and the vague outline you present to them - ignore their follow-up emails. Break off all communication with them until the idea is forgotten/the moment has passed.

7.

Make certain that you are never working on less than 12 to 20 projects at any one time. This is the safest way to ensure none of these projects will ever reach fruition – at the point one of them begins to show clear potential, it is essential to isolate this particular project: 'separate it from the pack'.

Spend time analysing it, looking for the weaknesses within it. A thorough analysis of these weaknesses will guarantee that this project remains 'just an idea', ensuring that, in time, it can be dismissed.

8.

It is crucial to work in many 'styles' - the adherence to a single recognisable style will inevitably lead to your output being associated with your name (think Yayoi Kusama, think Kraftwerk).

If this style gains acceptance, or worse, '<u>success</u>', you will effectively become a brand - for the Debrist, this is a <u>disaster</u>.[1]

1 It is tempting to think that one 'could always backtrack' from becoming a successful or 'signature' brand and assume a Debrist position within any of the arts, but this is not wholly true:

It is accepted knowledge that the third most difficult position for an artist to attain is the Cultural Gatekeeper's declaration of their 'genius' – 'genius' is, of course, an over-used (but still very rare) accolade – and if this accolade gains traction (especially internationally), the 'genius artist' is guaranteed both a lifetime's audience and (at the very least) a reasonable financial income.

The second most difficult position for an artist to attain is the Cultural Gatekeeper's labelling of their work as 'good', once their output has already been labelled as 'bad'. Labels stick and no amount of evidence to the contrary will reverse this decision. Consequently, the 'bad artist' must either accept their place in the lower rungs (or even outside edges) of their particular 'art world', disappear into academia, or – in extreme cases – relocate to a seaside town.

However, by far the most difficult position for any artist to negotiate is to have the Cultural Gatekeepers of their particular 'art world' label them a 'genius', and then for the 'genius artist' to attempt to prove that they are, in fact, quite the opposite. Shedding the 'genius' label is considered to be almost an impossibility: some artists have spent their entire careers attempting to escape an early institutional/international 'declaration of genius', struggling in vain to prove that they are in fact a mediocrity, or maybe even a 'bad artist' – but their efforts are usually in vain. To reiterate: labels stick – capital (both cultural and financial) has been invested – and no amount of wilfully blundering ineptness will reverse the 'genius decision', once it has been ruled. Only the most doggedly persistent'former-genius' has been able to prove themselves inept, undeserving or, in some cases, even 'bad' enough to have the 'genius' decision reversed. But, be warned – the Cultural Gatekeepers do not like it – they will fight back, loudly and repeatedly celebrating the now 'former-genius' artist's 'ground-breaking early work' in every format available.

In short, if the culture worker makes a commitment and enters into the murky realms of 'signature style', there is a grave danger of Debrism being lost to them, forever.

9.

The single greatest way to avoid 'success' is by making a <u>daily</u> 'to-do' list. The trick is to not include anything on this list that is 'achievable' - or, if you must include that which is achievable (e.g. reply to email from X), ensure you counter this with a multitude of tasks which are <u>unachievable</u> (e.g. write a novel, record 'the greatest album of all time', lose 30 kilos in weight).

WARNING: the daily list must remain just that. The true Debrist knows that impossibility is the key. In simple terms, your list must read:

Lose 30 kilos today.[2]

NOT

Lose 30 kilos this year.

2 The crucial role of 'unachievable goals' cannot be overstated enough in the practice of Debrism: though it is essential that YOU are utterly convinced by the achievability of your daily 'to-do' lists. 'Lose 30 kilos today' is of course an exaggeration made only to illustrate a point about the correct Debrist mindset. If you require a more practical example: think of a simple and 'achievable' task that you 'have been meaning to do for months' but that has proven impossible for you to execute (e.g. 'transfer desktop on to hard drive', 'clean fridge', 'go to Ikea'); then simply add that to your 'today's to-do list' – the failure to execute this task will ensure that you remain within the correct creative/frustrated mindset.

10.

Although Debris is primarily created by spending 'too much' time alone (and in a specific space or locale) – there is a great danger that success may follow if you isolate yourself with a clear goal.

For example: If the culture worker were to isolate themselves for months on end, spend 10 hours each day writing a novel (and had some aptitude for this), there is every chance that within six months to a year they would have a first/second draft novel of some insight and quality. Finding themselves in possession of a manuscript with genuine potential, they could then legitimately send it to 'writer friends' and publishers – i.e. there is a grave danger that they could be taken seriously. <u>This is a common mistake</u>.

In order to counter the threat of being taken seriously as a novelist/playwright/architect/painter/person, it is essential that you:

- Create the impression of yourself as someone who is thoroughly out of touch with 'the conversation'.

- Do not present yourself as unintelligent. This will lead to a complete breakdown of Debris production: your goal is not to attract hatred or trolling, but exclusion. You are simply being honest about your <u>genuine</u> passions and therefore proving yourself to be <u>irrelevant</u>.

- <u>TAKE ACTION</u>: if threatened with <u>inclusion</u>, the most immediate and effective action the Debrist can take is to be <u>honest</u>. If used sparingly, honesty is one of the greatest weapons you have at your disposal.

E.G. you could choose the wrong occasion on which to simply 'be yourself': in a rare conversation with a high-powered Cultural Gatekeeper, you might make it clear that you are infinitely more au fait with (for example) the best way to 'pull a wheelie' on a Suzuki GSX-R750 motorcycle – or – every single episode of the vintage TV show 'Bewitched', than you are with (for example) anything at all to do with Brian Eno, or the 'market implications' of the NFT boom... and you certainly aren't sure which 'politicised young art collectives' the Cultural Gatekeeper should 'check out'.

However, if – in a particular situation – you feel that honesty is perhaps not an effective policy, you do have a second tool at your disposal, and that is cultural democracy as praxis.

We live in a world where 'cultural worth', for too long, has been determined by a wealthy elite. And although most leading cultural institutions have latterly recognised – and taken some measures to correct this – have they really done enough?

As a Debrist, it is your duty to break-down the barriers between 'culture' (as an institutionally sanctioned preserve of the wealthy elite) and 'the people'. The Debrist, of course, recognises that an exciting haircut, or a brilliant T-shirt is at least as culturally valid as any gallery-based artwork/ book reading/minimalist score for a solo flautist. Indeed, the Debrist firmly believes that 'art' should be both 'for' and 'of' the people, and consequently is duty-bound to pioneer measures that embrace those who would ordinarily feel excluded from or intimidated by 'high culture'.

But how can this be achieved?

PROPOSITION:

With the promise of 'endless free drinks', why not repeatedly invite the (sometimes) friendly, alcoholic couple, who sit by your nearest ATM, into 'your world' (including: business lunches, book launches and gallery 'private views'). This will prove to your peers that you are infinitely more committed to cultural democracy as praxis than they are, while simultaneously – and in true Debrist fashion – also ensuring that you are excluded from receiving any further social/business invitations in the future.

11.
Un-networking is the single greatest friend of the Debrist.

PRODUCTION AND DISTRIBUTION

These 'Covid times' have made it easy for many would-be Debrists. Lockdown restrictions and the end of/minimizing of social occasions such as gallery openings, 'private screenings' and 'exclusive after-show parties' have led to a dramatic downturn in the opportunities culture workers would normally have to introduce themselves to Cultural Gatekeepers, in the hope that the gatekeeper might like their painting/writing/movie script/music/architecture.

In short, there is a current backlog of Debris (those who would normally be offered exhibitions/book deals/recording contracts etc. are also finding themselves isolated and unable to realize projects). They are, effectively, jamming up the natural Debris hierarchy. But, these 'accidental' or 'dilettante Debrists' are merely the unwitting beneficiaries of a temporary breakdown in the normal distribution circuits.

DO NOT DESPAIR

Just as there was a backlog of articulated trucks, queuing to get to the continent from the UK, in the immediate aftermath of the new 'Brexit rules' on import/export – so there will be an excess of Debris created by culture workers when international Covid restrictions are finally lifted. But, just as the trucks were eventually given papers and cleared to enter and unload their goods in continental Europe, so the backlog of faux-Debrists will clear, once the social mechanisms of the arts begin again. The excited meetings of artists/gallerists, and of writers/publishers, will quickly lead to the creative industries being back on their feet, and the world of gallery exhibitions, book launches etc. suddenly being in full flow. Within months, the world of arts will be fully functioning, just as it always was – the 'Covid nightmare' being reduced to a vague memory of enforced leisure – a déjà vu of limbo. In short, both the ordinary culture worker and the Cultural Gatekeeper will be raring to go, so excited by the possibilities of their new-found freedom that they may even wish to include YOU.

HOW CAN THE TRUE DEBRIST COUNTER THIS?

IT IS ESSENTIAL THAT THE DEBRIST PARTICIPATES ENTHUSIASTICALLY IN THESE RELAUNCHED SOCIAL/WORK GATHERINGS.

But only because, they must remind the:

- BOOK PUBLISHER
- EXHIBITING ARTIST
- MUSEUM DIRECTOR
- RECORD COMPANY BOSS
- CURATOR (VARIOUS)
- AGEING POP STAR
- FAMED JOURNALIST
- INDEPENDENT MOVIE PRODUCER
- SUCCESSFUL PLAYWRIGHT
- CEO OF LUXURY GOODS BRAND

& even...

- AMBITIOUS STUDENT/INTERN (POTENTIAL FUTURE ALLY)

That the Debrist is a social misfit, liability, fantasist and 'time-waster', as quickly and brutally as possible. What better forum or theatre to do this in, than in the giddy excitement of the first few weeks of the rapid boomerang of 'post-lockdown freedom'?

As with any Debrist tactic, one must be careful.

IMAGINE THIS SCENARIO:

Unusually, you are invited to the opening of a major museum retrospective celebrating a leading contemporary artist. You are not, of course, invited to 'the dinner' – that would be unthinkable. But even this invitation (to a semi-public 'private view') is as inconvenient as it is flattering.

I.E. for most ambitious culture workers such an invite would be considered an honour – but for the Debrist this is potentially a source of great personal trauma.

HOW TO TURN THIS NEGATIVE INTO A POSITIVE?

There are several possible solutions to this problem:

SOLUTION 1

Accept the invitation with good grace. R.S.V.P. immediately, being sure to say, "I would be very happy to attend." Look forward to the event, dress nicely (but casually), or the converse: over-the-top costumery. Be sure only to drink the minimum ('social') amount, and float around the event smiling and introducing yourself to as many Cultural Gatekeepers as possible. Be sure to tell them what it is you do, making sure you repeat (several times in their presence) your full name, and that "yes" you do know, and like very much, their good friend Matt/Anna/Francois/Matilde. Leave the event, having made a fantastic impression – ensure you go straight home, resisting the invitation to join your new friends for dinner/further drinks (the dangers of this being obvious).

SOLUTION 2

Ignore the invite – move it immediately to the 'trash' on your desktop, while simultaneously making sure your 'peers' are aware that you were in fact invited, you just did not want to go (you may wish to elaborate on your reasons for this – e.g. a previously undisclosed and 'more important' engagement).

SOLUTION 3

Plan to attend – even though such events fill you with dread. Let the event weigh heavily on your mind for days, maybe even weeks. Do not drink any alcohol in the meantime – tell yourself that this event will be the perfect excuse to let your hair down and enjoy yourself. In fact, use the time between now and the evening of the event to work around the clock: bury yourself in a spartan regime of long days, extreme sobriety, possibly even rigorous physical exercise – and certainly use the day of the event as the deadline on which you plan to 'finish' your latest project. On the day of the event you will be tired, and you may well be frustrated (a true Debrist having not only 'not finished their latest project', but also started a dozen more paintings/ novels/theatre plays). Make the day of the event/missed deadline one long celebration/release. The logic is simple: you are going to start drinking alcohol at the event, obviously – so what difference does it make? You know you will be consuming free champagne cocktails by 6.30pm, so why not start drinking at home, alone, at 12.30pm? It is your day off.

Arrive at the event early, only to realise you are in fact, the first person there. The shame. Leave quickly and go to the nearest bar. Here you can regroup and allow time for the other guests to arrive, the logic being that your arrival will then seem casual, maybe even a little 'disinterested'. Become far too comfortable drinking alone in the bar – one eye on the clock, promising yourself that the next drink will be your last. It is now 8.00pm – the event finishes at 8.30pm – you have been drinking heavily for over seven hours. Force yourself to go to the event – there is still half an hour left, and this is long enough for you to make a memorable impression.

Wake up the next morning in the hallway of your own home. Lie there for some time, comfortable at first, until you remember last night; when you verbally attacked a 'signature piece' by the leading contemporary artist, pointing at and loudly declaiming the celebrated sculpture – even trying to aim a flying kick at it – as his guests mingled in the museum foyer. The indignity of this is enormous: you see a fog of silent but screaming faces; the shocked expressions mirroring the havoc, misery and confusion you created, before nonchalant security staff marched you past the distressed friends and allies of the leading contemporary artist, and towards the EXIT.

Stop. Think. Reverse.

What would once have constituted an outright disaster is now an unequivocal triumph. Your behaviour was perfect: you are now – indisputably – a leading Debrist. You must be able to work in a vacuum, and what you achieved in only a matter of minutes last night has just bought you at least three years of freedom.

12.
Extraneous Threats

COLLABORATING WITH FELLOW DEBRISTS

This is usually a perfectly safe thing to do – for obvious reasons: if your would-be collaborator is a true Debrist they will have no more inclination towards finishing this joint/collaborative work than you do. The meetings you have in parks/bars/cafés will be totally harmless. You will discuss 'what we could do', there may even be moments of excitement as you realise that you are both currently obsessed by the same social mores/political posturing/historical minutiae. This is a danger, of course and could – disastrously – lead to some kind of 'collaboration'. But do not panic. The chances are, if your fellow Debrist is as committed as you are, your collaboration will never get off the ground.

THERE ARE MANY COMMON REASONS FOR THIS–

Most Debrists are perfectionists. This seems unlikely and even implausible to the non-Debrist (if they were to study the output of the Debrist), but it is true. The Debrists' insecurity and loss of confidence is mostly driven by the 'search for perfection' – in short: an impossible desire. And this 'search for perfection' inevitably leads to the abandonment of yesterday's 'breakthrough idea'. Why?

With any 'brand new approach', any 'major change in position', there is a huge chance of humiliation/failure. This is unacceptable to the Debrist/perfectionist, even when they are working alone.

So, if the Debrist is forced to collaborate, the chances of a true Debrist believing that 'someone else's idea is better than mine' – or even letting 'someone else contribute to my brilliant idea' – are so slim, that there is virtually no hope of your collaborative project being realised.

THUS...

It is perfectly safe to plan to collaborate with a fellow Debrist. Nothing will come of it. Interest will soon dissipate (as your idea becomes the dominant one) and your fellow Debrist will quickly retreat to the safety of their own home/laptop/chair.

However, a word of CAUTION:

Not all Debrists are as committed as you are. Some of them are merely 'slightly perfectionist', or worse, 'ambitious'. These kinds of collaborators must be avoided at all costs.

If you find yourself in a situation where you are about to begin a collaboration with a faux-Debrist, what are the signs?

The signs of a non-committed Debrist are many, though sometimes subtle. But if you notice any of the following traits in your would-be collaborator – walk away immediately:

1) A GENUINE DEADLINE SCENARIO, IN WHICH THEY CONTACT YOU VIA EMAIL:

> hey – i emailed nora (the curator) and she is really into this idea.
> she said that there is still a slot in this year's festival. so that's great![3]
> and she loved the title!
>
> i told her you had an idea about using a digital screen (seems there may be a cost issue here!!!)... but all good.
>
> nora said if we can get a script + costing to her by monday,
> they would love to have us in the festival!
>
> let's meet/zoom tomorrow. sound like a plan? ;-)

3 WARNING - The use of exclamation marks is always a giveaway to the bureaucratic manoeuvres of time-management and is now endemic in (written) digital communication:

! = I am your friend

!!! = Don't shoot the messenger

;-) = I aim to make you hate me so much that you will drop out of this project, and I can take all the glory for myself.

2) THE OTHER, VERY TELLING SIGN, OF A FAUX/SEMI- OR EVEN NON-DEBRIST IS A WILLINGNESS TO 'WORK OFF THEIR OWN BACK'. THIS COULD TAKE MANY FORMS, BUT BELOW IS AN OBVIOUS AND EASY TO UNDERSTAND EXAMPLE:

For many years you have been secretly working on 'spoken word' recordings. You imagine these being released one day, perhaps as an 'LP'. But it is of course, just a fantasy – in reality the very idea of your words/thoughts/true-feelings being committed to vinyl fills you with horror: your innermost self being laid bare for analysis/criticism/unintended hilarity or even genuine pleasure. But stupidly, just last week, you mentioned the recordings to a musician friend. He was shocked and surprisingly excited. He insisted that you send him the recordings, so you do. Nothing wrong with that, you have known him for many years, and he promises to keep them to himself.

Then the musician friend calls you. He uses his <u>voice</u> to communicate with you – surely a warning sign in itself – no sane person does this anymore. You are flustered and confused when you answer; he tells you that the recordings you have made are 'genius'. Your confusion is now crushed by your own dormant ego. When was the last time anyone said that something you did was 'genius'? You <u>cannot</u> remember.

Now on a high, and believing every word the musician says about your previously untapped brilliance as a 'spoken word artist', you agree to everything he suggests. He will "put some sounds to these". "Not make them into songs!" you hastily insist, and he assures you, "No, just some atmospherics, just add to them a bit, edit them and add some footsteps and stuff, maybe a bit of keyboards." You agree, flattered by his interest and curious to see what he will do. Then the icing on the cake: he says, "If it works out well, I'll play them to my record company, see what they think." Now <u>extremely</u> flattered, and even mildly excited, you ask yourself: "What harm could it do?" An error on your part.

FOR THE NEXT WEEK YOU CANNOT SLEEP. YOU RUN THROUGH THE POSSIBILITIES, BOTH GOOD AND BAD:

A) He won't do anything. It was all talk. He was probably stoned or drunk, or both.

B) I cannot stand his music. It is shit. And his 'record label' is just one bloke in a bedroom in Finchley. This is potentially the most humiliating thing I have ever done.

C) Maybe they will be great. Maybe I have found my way at last. Maybe I will be the star of next year's South by Southwest festival. I will go on tour – I will have a voice. I will have my own TV show.

D) I will tell him I have changed my mind.

E) Then, BINGO...

You remember who you are – you remember, proudly, what you are. You are a leading Debrist and you will get Debrist on him.

You contact your musician friend. You call him by voice, hoping to cause the same communication blitzkrieg in his mind that he caused in yours. You will shock him with an early morning call.

You tell him:

"I'm not really happy with most of those recordings. In fact, all of them need a bit of work."

He tells you:

"You're joking. They're great!"

He seems unfazed by both your early morning call and unexpected use of voice. You have to dig in:

"No. If we're going to do this, I want to do it properly. I'm really not entirely comfortable with some of the words I used..."

And before you can say anything else, he says:

"I can just drop in the word changes. Come down to the studio and we will do it tomorrow."

This takes you aback – this so-called friend is no Debrist. The double betrayal of doing something for someone else, and worse, attempting to make a specific and clear appointment of when and where, is more than you can stand.

"I am really <u>not</u> happy with them yet," you say, trying to be both authoritative and calm.

"Oh," he says, disappointed.

So you go in for the kill. You hope to expose him as a true and loyal fellow Debrist:

"I don't suppose you've done anything with the recordings yet?"

"No not yet," he says, "I will though."

You breathe a sigh of relief. Your friend is a Debrist after all – though maybe not to your level – so this is a crucial moment. If you give him even the slightest encouragement, he might start today, adding footsteps and ambience to your embarrassing words. You cut him dead.

"Let me just make a few changes," you tell him. "I'll send the recordings to you by the end of this week."[4]

4 Though I continuously refer to the 'world of the arts', you might equally apply these examples to office or factory work. Remember – the goal is not to be involved, to create <u>time that is your own</u> – in order to pursue your true calling: Debrism. You may be a junior copywriter in an advertising agency, consistently neglecting the projects you are set in order to use 'their time' to work on your first anthology of poetry. You may be the assistant manager in a fast-food outlet, ignoring customer complaints in order to write lyrics for the band in which you will be the lead singer. You may be a once-ambitious estate agent who uses 'their time' to develop your first cosmetics range, etc.

He accepts. The fool. You will never send him the revised recordings, and you will never give him your blessing to work on the ones he's got. He is trapped. CHECKMATE.

So... although the Debrist is often threatened by would-be collaborators, the true Debrist will always resist.

NEVER FORGET:
'Casual collaboration' (as threatened by a friend or acquaintance) - is a smiling assassin in the world of Debrism.

The threat of publishing/exhibiting/collaborating can unnerve the Debrist. 'Publishing' and 'exhibiting' are threats that will dissipate over time: the more committed the Debrist, the less chance they have of encountering these external threats. It is your determination to prove that you cannot commit to or finish anything that will, in the long run, protect you from this kind of exposure.

As noted: collaboration is a tricky field to negotiate – and, although it is not exceptionally difficult to quash the collaborative ambitions of an unsuccessful musician friend...

How does one dissuade the threat of collaboration if proposed by a professional person or body?

'Professional collaboration' requires a much firmer hand.

CONSIDER THE EXAMPLE AND SOLUTION BELOW:

You have a brilliant idea... This is not unusual - as a leading Debrist, you have almost nothing but brilliant ideas.

Pleased with your latest idea and convinced of its commercial potential, you seek advice from a former colleague. She suggests you contact her friend who is 'an expert in this field', and may even want to 'collaborate'. Your former colleague reassures you that her friend is 'highly respected and works with Hollywood stars'. This of course, sets alarm bells ringing, but you contact this person regardless. He is friendly, if an obsequious name-dropper. He is very interested in your 'brilliant idea', and tells you he would 'potentially love to be involved'. Later that day he emails you with 'just a few questions':

- What is your marketing strategy for this?
- Will it be exhibited anywhere?
- How many do you plan to sell?
- Finished design: can my team see ASAP?
- Can you send over the press release?
- Timescale: going forward, can you advise on a ballpark schedule?

This, of course, is deeply unnerving. A direct threat, not only of collaboration, but of presumed, if not even almost guaranteed success.

WHAT TO DO?

You must reply to his email:

Not immediately, but at an unusual time. 4.30 a.m. is a good time to counter this kind of highly organised, professional threat. Why?

BECAUSE IT SUGGESTS THAT:

A) You may have been up all night, possibly drinking, or worse.

Or, infinitely less likely:

B) You get up so insanely early that you may be a loose cannon, a self-employed despot, so ambitious that you hardly ever sleep.

Either way, it is essential to dissipate the threat in a single email: nip it in the bud before any further conversation can take place.

BUT HOW?

The 'excessively sorry' strategy is by far the safest and most efficient approach. In the politest possible terms, make clear to your enthusiastic, would-be collaborator:

- There is no press release.
- There is no marketing plan.
- There is no product, it is just an idea.

The way you phrase this is crucial: ensure to be apologetic. This will unnerve your 'go-getter' would-be collaborator. Punctuate your reply heavily with the word 'sorry' – create an image of yourself as a humble fantasist, a subservient imbecile clearly out of your depth, ashamed that you even dared to contact such a 'professional' would-be collaborator. They will not pity you; they will fleetingly despise you. But, crucially, they will quickly forget you and never reply.

That was a close shave. Do not worry – you can soon return to unadulterated Debris production. But first, you must reacquaint yourself with this...

13.
The Basics of Debrism: A Refresher

1. FAILURE IS SUCCESS

Fear of failure[5] was once the motivator. Reverse that – fear of success is the motivator.

Failure is success in art (and life): desire[6] is everything.

However: desire must not be so great that a willingness to complete/ compete arises.

By first admitting failure, we cannot fail – this is not negativity – this is the Debrist dialectic.[7]

5 Case study: "My whole adult life has been one endless stream of anxiety because I have constantly sought out 'perfection', and of course, I have failed, as anyone would." The seeking of 'perfection' is an action that is engineered to fail: 'I am not good enough', 'This is not good enough', 'You are not good enough', 'Nothing is good enough', etc.

6 We pursue only conceptual cul-de-sacs – as the cul-de-sac has no exit, we can neither find it, nor fail to find it – but we must embrace it.

7 The admission of 'failure' before any action takes place – i.e. 'This will fail'; 'This is pointless'; 'This is terrible' – is the correct stance for the committed Debrist. Inevitably there will be moments of 'doubt' – i.e. 'But I am a great talent, therefore I will eventually "succeed"' – these thoughts – when they occur – must be made composite – i.e. 'I will succeed in creating a new failure'.

2. MAXIMIZE FRUSTRATION

Remember that feeling you used to have before an idea[8] was resolved? You used to call it 'frustration'. It used to create self-doubt. But now, you live permanently in the zone of self-doubt. This is incredibly healthy. Nothing is or can ever be resolved – certainly not the image itself. If you were to solve this particular problem, what would await you? Another problem. Therefore there is very little point in ever resolving the current problem: it is this process (and the wisdom gained from it), that over time, comes to define the Debrist.

8 'Unsuccessful' art-making (of any kind) should only ever adhere to 'singular solution seeking' (a coherence of signs = sum = logic). Do NOT attempt to engage with either 'the language of art', 'the language of popular music' or 'the language of poetry' – i.e. car crash semiotics. Why? *Car crash semiotics = multiple readings = viewer access = 'open to interpretation' = mirror = 'correct interpretation' = success (i.e. failure); furthermore: success = joy + power + confidence = SATISFACTION = the most potent force of anti-Debrism.*

3. PURSUE PERFECTIONISM

THE BOUNDLESS CREATION OF THOUGHT AND SURPLUS IS OUR AIM.
WE SEEK ONLY PERFECTION.
WE PURSUE THE IMPOSSIBILITY OF 'THE MASTERPIECE':
BECAUSE WE AIM TO BE IGNORED.

Perfectionism is not the enemy. Perfectionism is the sign of the obsessive, the addict, the seeker. Embrace perfectionism to the highest degree – pure perfectionism is our greatest weapon – nothing will ever be decided, nothing will ever be complete, nothing will ever be made.

The pursuit of perfection is a wilful enterprise of creative self-destruction – comparable to the Japanese samurai act of 'Seppuku' (suicide by disembowelment). We are fully aware of this, and embrace it wholly.

4. ABOLISH FORM

Consider the ancient maxims below:

A) "THE IDEA BECOMES THE MACHINE THAT MAKES THE ART"
– Sol LeWitt

And correct it:

THE IDEA DOES NOT BECOME THE MACHINE THAT MAKES THE ART:

THE IDEA
BECOMES
THE IDEA
BECOMES
THE IDEA
BECOMES
THE IDEA
BECOMES
THE IDEA
BECOMES
Repeat *ad infinitum*

Or, more accurately, within the discipline of Debrism:

THE THOUGHT IS
THE THOUGHT IS
THE THOUGHT IS
THE THOUGHT IS
THE THOUGHT IS
THE THOUGHT IS
THE THOUGHT IS
THE THOUGHT IS
THE THOUGHT IS
THE THOUGHT IS
THE THOUGHT IS
THE THOUGHT IS
THE THOUGHT IS
THE THOUGHT IS
THE THOUGHT IS
Repeat *ad infinitum*

Should a thought become so powerful that it begins to manifest itself as 'an idea', the Debrist must act immediately[9]. Ideas, if made public at any stage, may threaten to become fully formed – or worse – may attract an external threat (in the form of a commission or similar) – i.e. there is a very real danger here that your thought/idea might well find a context and even be made 'concrete'.

Thoughts are inevitable, as are ideas. The question is, what does the Debrist do with them? There is only one solution:

Once a thought threatens to metamorphosize into an idea, take action. You must subject the fledgling idea to such intense scrutiny that any natural flaw within it (e.g. lack of conceptual rigidity) is exposed. A thorough analysis of this flaw will, in time, result in the 'invalidation' of the idea – i.e. safely returning it to its previous theoretical status of being 'just a thought'.

B) "IDEAS ALONE CAN BE WORKS OF ART; THEY ARE IN A CHAIN OF DEVELOPMENT THAT MAY EVENTUALLY FIND SOME FORM. ALL IDEAS NEED NOT BE MADE PHYSICAL."
– Sol LeWitt

My underlining: although the American artist Sol LeWitt could – in many respects – have claimed to be the father of 'Conceptual art', both his much admired 'Paragraphs on Conceptual Art' (*Artforum*, 1967), and his lesser known 'Sentences on Conceptual Art' (*Art-Language*, 1969) are seriously undermined from a Debrist perspective by:

i) LeWitt's references to 'form' – these completely undermine any claim that the deceased artist might also have been 'The Father of Debrism' [what LeWitt was suggesting was akin to a 'conceptual' or ideas-driven art Fordism: the compartmentalising of 'concept' as part of a manufacturing process, in which 'ideas' are the blueprint for a product that would, sooner or later ("may eventually"), take some physical form].

ii) LeWitt repeatedly insists on referring to 'ideas': the true Debrist is much more likely to use the term 'thoughts' or 'just a thought', than the inherently doctrinal 'ideas'.

9 The Debrist knows this, and consequently feels absolutely no obligation to make either 'a thought' or (the much more ambitious) 'an idea' concrete (i.e. give it form). Neither does the Debrist feel any obligation whatsoever to make 'the thought' public, nor to 'upgrade' that thought to the status of 'an idea'. See: POINT 7 in main manifesto.

5. EMBRACE THE JOURNEY

In its least successful form Debrism is the creation of by-product (cultural landfill) – but – in its purest form, Debrism is the ceaseless search for 'direction' within the confines of late Anthropocene 'surveillance capitalism'.[10]

In your pre-Debrist days, you were employed by Cultural Gatekeepers to 'create solutions' to their 'problems' – this gave you not only a strong sense of purpose (and completion), but also an income.

However, the major issue most under-employed culture workers now face is that they continue to 'create solutions', without first being handed a problem (e.g. the culture worker may continue to create artwork for album covers they have not been commissioned to design, attempt to write novels that will never be published, contemplate their contribution to a 'group show' in which they have not been invited to participate etc.).

To clarify, the mental state of the under-employed culture worker (prior to their initiation into Debrism), is perhaps best illustrated by imagining the following situation:

10 "Surveillance capitalism unilaterally claims human experience as free raw material for translation into behavioural data. Although some of these data are applied to service improvement, the rest are declared as a proprietary behavioural surplus..."
– Shoshana Zuboff, The *Age of Surveillance Capitalism: The Fight for a Human Future at the New Frontier of Power* (Profile Books, 2019).

THINK OF YOURSELF IN AN OLD MERCEDES CAR, HIGH POWERED, ONCE-BEAUTIFUL, NOW RUSTED AND BROKEN – THE ENGINE REVVING CRAZILY AS YOU FLOOR THE ACCELERATOR AGAIN AND AGAIN. THINK OF THIS CAR PARKED IN YOUR STREET – IT IS SUNDAY MORNING, BUT YOU HAVE BEEN SITTING HERE WITH YOUR FOOT HARD ON THE ACCELERATOR, AROUND THE CLOCK, FOR MANY WEEKS. YOUR NEIGHBOURS CANNOT SLEEP. THE CAR IS PERMANENTLY STUCK IN NEUTRAL, REVVING LOUDER AND LOUDER. STUCK FOREVER AS THE BIG ENGINE ROARS AND WHINES – SO LOUDLY – THE ACCELERATOR <u>STAMPED</u> HARD TO THE FLOOR. THIS DEAFENING DIN HAS ONLY ONE PURPOSE – IT BLOCKS OUT YOUR SCREAMS.

But – do not despair – Debrism is merely an attitude, and the correct Debrist mindset is one of 'Zen-like' acceptance. Banish all thoughts of 'arrival' from your mind and embrace the journey.

Put more literally:

Continue to seek out 'solutions', by all means. Try to 'find your way', try to make your mark – this effort is at the very heart of Debrism and it must be encouraged.

Do sit at your desk and rack your brains.

But do NOT ask yourself:

"HOW CAN I MAKE THIS THOUGHT AN IDEA?"
"HOW CAN I GET THIS IDEA MADE?"
"HOW CAN I IMPRESS THEM?"
"HOW CAN I HAVE A 'HIT'?"

Because:

The answer is – YOU CAN'T.

Not if you wish to remain a Debrist.

6. EMBRACE THE VOID

We do not 're-contextualise' – we aim to de-contextualise, fully aware that this is impossible. (Refuse history. Seek only to mirror the present.[11] With no critical, ironic or intellectual commentary). Ambiguity and cognitive dissonance are key.

We do not seek glory. Glory is the goal of the obsessive, weak, 'individual', who seeks only to mythologise their own delicate and questionable 'individuality'. Our aim is endless pursuit – we do not seek the blessing of others, we do not seek endorsement, celebration, completion or distribution.

11 'The present' is a deeply ambiguous term. There are many 'presents'. The isolated steam railway enthusiast is no less 'in the present' than the most vocal technology-obsessed conspiracy theorist. Debrism allows – even encourages – the pursuit of personal obsessions which have no meaning to others and no status (anti-status, even) in a world where culture workers are encouraged primarily only to broadcast 'empathy'. The further the Debrist pursues 'the wrong kind of obsession' the safer they are from social acceptance/celebration – and although the Debrist might think they are safe in choosing to engage wholeheartedly with 'obsessions' that the Cultural Gatekeeper considers to be invalid by 'cliché' (e.g. a preoccupation with 'punk rock' being a good example [though be warned: certain 'punk rock' bands are considered to be almost 'above cliché' – one such example being now defunct Manchester (UK) band, The Fall]), there is no guarantee that the subject/form your output embraces will necessarily be considered 'clichéd' – for example, the Cultural Gatekeeper may mistake your use of tired subject matter and meaningless materials as 'ironic'. In short, it is best – safest – to stick rigidly to the pursuit of thoughts/ideas, never making them public unless absolutely necessary.

7. WORSHIP THE MASTERPIECE

We firmly believe in the concept of 'The Masterpiece'[12] in all its forms. We believe it is our duty to attempt to create 'The Masterpiece' on a daily basis. We believe the creation of 'The Masterpiece' to be an impossibility.

8. INDIVIDUALISM AT ALL COSTS

We seek self-fulfilment through our own actions, we are only reliant on others as either:

A) The friends of Debris (high-powered Cultural Gatekeepers)

Or

B) The enemies of Debris (independent structures, small record companies, obscure literary festivals, bespoke publishing houses, unfashionable art galleries, certain charity auctions, etc.)

12 We fully understand that 'The Masterpiece' is an institutional construct, and that this 'honour' can only be bestowed on a work of art/music/literature by a collective international agreement brokered by Cultural Gatekeepers and their pay-masters – but 'pointless pursuit' is the engine that drives all Debrist ideology.

9. THE MIRROR

All commodity ('end product') is MIRROR[13] – a reflection of how the would-be consumer wishes to see themselves. Consequently, as previously noted: we vehemently oppose 'end product'.

13 Art as Mirror: Imagine you are rich, imagine you collect art. You fly to the art fair* – where the gallery booths are staffed by stylish and charming young people. You look at the work, you wander around for a while, until eventually, you come back to the first piece – the one that 'drew you in'. You like this one, you stand and gaze. It has no 'obvious narrative', not quite – it is abstract (or, it is, most likely: a confusion of signs). It is beautiful, an enigma, a puzzle. A member of the gallery staff sees you – you've been there some time. You ask: "What is this about?" Then, before they can answer, you boldly say, "Because it seems to me to be about... It reminds me of... And I see in it..." The staff member smiles and tells you, "Yes! You are absolutely right." You feel intelligent – you knew you understood. You decide to buy this work there and then – a memento to this moment – this recognition: a reminder to yourself of your own perceptual prowess. You knew you were right, of course you were right...

Because: what you were looking at was a mirror.† What you were offered was a loose collection of signifiers that do not make a singular sign. This is important: the signifiers do construct a 'sign', but they do not construct a singular sign. You were not looking at a commercial advertising billboard: there was no a) unusual but attractive image that b) began to make sense once you'd read the large headline and c) mentally linked the image to this headline that d) made absolute sense once you'd seen the pack shot/brand logo in the bottom right of the billboard. You were not looking at a simple (if lightly coded) singular message. You were looking at a smorgasbord of signifiers, and, consequently, there is no 'correct reading'. That is how you came to be so triumphantly correct – because your interpretation is – in most cases – just as good as the next customer's – and this fluidity, this modularity – this equation - plays no small part in keeping the business that they call 'the art world' moving.‡

* Art fair: mostly (temporarily) online, this is a historical example.

† Narcissus: in Greek mythology, Narcissus (nárkissos) was a hunter from Thespiae in Boeotia who was known for his beauty. According to Tzetzes, he rejected all romantic advances, eventually falling in love with his own reflection in a pool of water. He later died, and in his place sprouted the museum that bears his name.

‡ See Umberto Eco's *The Role of the Reader* (Indiana University Press,1979): all text is open. All art is open. "The notion of a crystal-like textual object is cast in doubt"; "It is just by playing upon the prerequisites of such general process that a text can succeed in being more or less open or closed".

10. NEGATE THEORY

It is very tempting to be fooled by other people's theories and philosophies – it is common practice for 'artists' (and writers, and architects, though less common amongst musicians)[14] to publicly allude to (claim) or appropriate particular philosophers and thinkers as 'their own': ideological limpets, clinging to the side of someone else's swimming pool – the favourites once being Deleuze and Guattari, or Silvia Federici, and more recently Mark Fisher (or even – still – Ballard, for those with less intellect… and desperately in need of an exhibition title).

It is essential that you never align yourself to a recognised/serious thinker. Your open affiliation will lead ONLY to acceptance – possibly even the invitation to join a faction – or, in the worst-case scenario: take part in a symposium.

Much better to create – and keep secret – your own philosophy. That way nobody will ever know what it is you are actually doing – and most crucially you will remain invisible to 'the critic'.[15]

14 Within the tradition of Western mainstream/popular music there are ONLY two philosophical (read: religious) positions to choose from: the protagonist/singer/whole band must either present themselves as an 'Agent of God', or as an 'Agent of the Devil'. Although there are many variations – and sometimes even subtleties – within this formula (e.g. the protagonist is often 'torn' between their allegiance to one side or the other), there are, ultimately, no exceptions to this rule.

15 How not to appeal to the critic: the professional critic – like any other social media 'influencer' – seeks to align themself with kudos. This is their primary motivation – kudos (i.e. 'getting it right' – getting it 'the same' [as their fellow critics] – adhering to consensus) is the only thing that keeps the critic in a position of power; consequently, the critic lives in perpetual fear – e.g. "Can I really be the first to point out that this beloved 'bard of the street' isn't actually from a working-class background?… because if I do, someone might point out that (by definition of my job) I'm no longer working class either… the flashlight of authenticity shone brightly in my face instead of theirs… is it worth it? No." So, while retaining the power to authenticate/inauthenticate your output in a single flurry of their laptop keyboard, the critic – troubled by their own insecurities and need to fit in, is best avoided completely – i.e. if you wish to continue your work as a committed Debrist, it is crucial that you remain firmly off-radar to the critic. But how? It is quite simple: project a 'lack of seriousness'.

A 'lack of seriousness' can of course take many forms – and it is essential that you remember, this is not a genuine lack of seriousness; this is simply a seeming lack of seriousness. An 'image' you are wilfully constructing in order to be ignored.

By far the best way to project a convincing lack of seriousness is via social media.

11. UNDERSTANDING SOCIAL MEDIA

The Debrist – if more confident – would be inclined to avoid social media in all its forms, and although this is tempting, a self-imposed negation of the current modes of communication could be counterproductive: the use of social media, if nothing else, does serve to remind the Cultural Gatekeeper that they have no interest in you whatsoever.

The culture worker who has no social media presence also runs the risk of creating an aura of aloofness, perhaps even mystery: the great danger here of course is 'attraction', and in the worst-case scenario, offers of collaboration or even commission.

So although the Debrist will never be an assertive user of social media – often editing or even deleting posts – it is essential that they maintain at least a token visibility.

With this in mind the Debrist needs to consider their 'social media profile'.

It goes without saying that your leanings are liberal or 'leftist', but how seriously should one commit to being publicly vocal about current events?

Seriousness is slippery and ever evolving, but only in its detail (read: subject matter). A standard-level seriousness can be applied to all matters of current concern. How you choose to project your 'personal' (constructed) attitude to whatever the current hot topic of concern is, is a delicate operation: too much shared concern (filtered through Instagram, for example) and you will become 'overly-involved' – this is a disaster for the Debrist. However, displaying too little concern is even more dangerous, and may eventually lead to complete ostracization (eliminating all 'hope': the very heart of Debrism). So, it is essential that the Debrist engineers their position carefully.

Put simply, there are four basic public personae that other social media users will assign to you:

- 'ACTIVIST'
- 'EMPATHISER'
- 'APATHIST'[16]
- 'NAZI'

The majority of culture workers would appear to fit neatly into one of the first three categories – this makes them very easy to understand, but

also somewhat invalidates their position as an 'authentic' (believable/ complex) human being. The Debrist – of course – must never fit squarely into any category – certainly not the extremities of 'Activist' or 'Nazi' – no, the true Debrist most likely chooses to float between 'Empathiser' and 'Apathist' – sometimes closer to one than the other, depending on who they are speaking to at the time. This is the ideal position for the working Debrist: showing both a seeming lack of commitment and an unwillingness to be pigeon-holed or 'counted' (i.e. involved in what for some – but not all – culture workers is undoubtedly a theatre of tokenism), while simultaneously showing (a sometimes genuine) concern for those issues that they actually do feel quite strongly about.

So long as the Debrist can continuously drift between 'empathy' and 'apathy', they will not be tethered by commitment, and are therefore free to continue Debris production, without the distraction of real-imagined-projected-politik.[17]

16 Be cautious when floating between categories – although it is essential to your freedom that you are never pinned down or labelled, do not make the mistake of wandering carelessly 'below' apathy, where there is a distinct possibility that you may be wrongly labelled an 'Apathist Nazi'.

REMEMBER: 'Fluid commitment' is the key. Let others take sides on the social media battlefield, where the chances are your protest reaches only your 'followers' (who already agree with you) – your protestations trapped into a circular agreement of ♥'s/mutual support/identity confirmation.

17 Fear of Language - The Debrist must be ever-vigilant before making any opinion public. So, if you must be 'part of the conversation' – even if only to remind others that you are still present/working – be sure to carefully check what the consensus of opinion is (before strongly supporting that consensus of opinion). Again, do not be overly aggressive – do not presume it is safe to use phrases of your own (if you must use phrases at all – see following chapter).

12. EMPATHY WITHOUT COMMITMENT

By far the safest method for expressing 'empathy' (without commitment), is simply to ❤️ an Instagram post that has already been safely ❤️'ed by leading culture workers and members of the public alike. Do not get carried away – thinking that this 'post' (most likely authored by a Cultural Gatekeeper or similar, regarding an important international concern) is the forum for you to voice a unique opinion: the danger of using the incorrect words is a very real and ever evolving threat (i.e. what may clearly be read as witty and insightful support today, could be seen as flippant and careless use of language tomorrow). If you cannot restrict yourself to the simple addition of a '❤️', then do feel free to add between x1 and x5 'emojis' that support the feeling/sentiment you wish to project – but again, do not be cavalier in your choice of emojis: because each of these symbols has an inherently clear and specific meaning – and even though a grouping of these symbols may read one way to you – they may not read like this to others.[18] Much better to copy an emoji pattern you have seen used successfully on a similar topic elsewhere, than it is to invent your own.

REMEMBER: this is a very public space – and getting it wrong could be disastrous for the Debrist. Your goal is to be largely ignored – you do not wish to become a target for trolls and 'haters'; nor do you wish to be recruited into the ranks of the 'Activist'.[19]

18 Digital Syntax:
❤️⚡🙂🎀👍 = I agree
💖💥😀🎀👊 = I strongly agree
💕🔥😁✝️👏 = I very strongly agree
😍💯🤩💫🙌 = I love everything you say regardless of what it is

19 TIP FOR USING INSTAGRAM – Instagram is essentially an updated and digitised re-modelling of the old 1970s 'lapel pin badge' communication system. So, if you are in doubt, and you are old enough to remember 'pin badges': before committing yourself to posting an image/comment, think, 'If this image/comment were a pin badge on my lapel, what would it say about me?'

14.
The future of Debrism is entirely reliant on NEW space.

For many years, the fully-functioning culture worker meticulously adhered to the creation/approval system that granted access to SPACE (gallery exhibitions, book deals, record releases, commissions, in-depth interviews etc.) – and the culture worker saw no reason to challenge this.

WHY WOULD THEY?

The semi-successful culture worker could easily convince themselves that this system was a meritocracy (of sorts): the best output = the best/most SPACE – and although there are many micro-divisions within the reflected status of any allocated SPACE, the pursuit of SPACE was seen to be 'the job' (legitimising the pursuit of brilliance [The Masterpiece/The New Way], while simultaneously augmenting THE FEAR OF FAILURE that drove the culture worker).

BECAUSE...

More than simply being in search of SPACE, the culture worker was in fact in search of the RIGHT SPACE ('<u>authenticating context</u>')[20]: the desperate desire to be 'needed' in Berlin, not Basingstoke; the desperate desire to be published, not 'self-published'; the desperate desire to be ceaselessly – digitally – 'present'.

Consequently, every culture worker, regardless of their (reflected) status, is locked into this endless search for the RIGHT SPACE on a dizzying multitude of levels: a space in which to be 'acknowledged', a space in which to be heard, a space in which to progress, and so on.

This is normal – and while the low-ranking culture worker might continue to 'look up' in envy at the seemingly RIGHT SPACE, in which their (former) peer's work recently appeared – they can also, without too much difficulty,

20 The 'RIGHT SPACE' (authenticating context) is, of course, so extremely rare that even the suggestion of 'A SPACE' (a context) can induce 'panic production' amongst culture workers: perfectly illustrated recently by their increasingly desperate attempts to benefit from the NFT 'gold rush'.

imagine their own output gracing a similar – if less distinguished – 'authenticating context' in the near future...

OR – failing that, at least take some comfort from the insider-knowledge that their former peer was not fully satisfied with the recently allocated 'authenticating context': a museum show, yes – but in San Francisco, not New York; a prestigious 'book deal', yes – but quietly funded by the high-ranking culture worker themselves, etc.

This endless pursuit of MORE, is normal for both high and low-ranking culture workers alike: the need for MORE being the only goal.

But what happens when the culture worker is denied SPACE to such a degree – that eventually – their every outlet seems to be blocked? Their once legitimate expectation of (at least some) SPACE now reduced to a faint hope – the once seemingly endless flow of 'proposals expected to be made concrete' slowly but systematically, and over a number of years, being first reduced to 'just some ideas', and finally to 'only a thought'?

At this point, the (now) dispossessed culture worker seems to be left with only two choices:

A) GIVE UP.
B) 'MOVE AWAY'.[21]

21 Those struggling with addiction often contemplate 'doing a geographical' – the idea being that a 'move away' (from the current environment) will prompt 'a brand-new start'; all the problems left behind in the old place. The culture worker equivalent of this – perhaps – being the move to a seaside town, or maybe an ex-mill town (with quaint cottages): a 'geographical' to a formerly working class/blue collar environment, where cheap property prices, boarded up shops and a less critical audience acted as a magnet to the disillusioned culture workers who pioneered the Mumfordisation* of this area; transforming it into an arts/crafts/fromagerie hotspot.

* Mumfordised / (see also *Mumfordisation*): Describing the successful transformation of a once rundown urban area/pit village/seaside town into a rural idyll. Mumfordisation most commonly begins with a single (non-chain) coffee shop acting as a nucleus, around which other businesses spring up— vintage and cycling shops, real ale pubs, rustic cafes — until the whole area is transformed (2014).

but

There is also a third, more powerful, option open to the culture worker: DEBRISM

In which:

YOU DO NOT NEED TO MAKE 'THE IDEA' CONCRETE.
YOU DO NOT NEED AN 'AUTHENTICATING CONTEXT'.
YOU DO NOT NEED APPROVAL OF ANY KIND.

Because, while the dispossessed culture worker lived only for the 'breakthrough moment' – and willingly pursued a thousand blind alleys, in the hope of 'finding their way' – the DEBRIST lives only to be lost:

DESTINATION CANCELLED.[22]

22 Pat and Bernie go to Lake George every year on vacation. Bernie is now 64, Pat is 63 – they dream of moving to live by the beautiful lake when Bernie retires. This is what has kept them going. They have dreamt of this ever since they first started coming here, when Bernie was 46 and Pat was 45. They love it here. Bernie will retire in a few months: the firm have confirmed this. So, now they visit Lake George, house-hunting, as often as they can – they seem to be here almost every weekend. It is becoming real now: the dream at last fulfilled. Pat and Bernie have money – they can buy a nice house near (or maybe even on) Lake George itself. In fact, they stand on a long green lawn by the lake right now, looking back at a beautiful clapboard house; it was immediately obvious, this house was the one. Not only does it overlook Lake George, it even has a wooden patio – almost a jetty really, that reaches right out into the famous lake. At sunset, and knowing that this is heaven, their dream come true, they hold hands. Thirty-seven years they've been together, bad times and good, but at last, the reward. Bernie says to Pat, "Well, honey, this is it, looks like we are home." Bernie then smiles at Pat – this is 'the moment'. "Shall we sign?" She asks Pat, "make it official?" Pat looks out across the lake – into the distance, at the mountains – her face bathed in the amber sunset, beatific. Her dream almost now true. Pat turns to her wife, her face suddenly concerned. "Bernie, darling," she says, "if we move here, where will we go on vacation?"

This is a great relief for the culture worker turned Debrist, who can now:

PUT ASIDE ALL THOUGHTS OF ARRIVAL ('THE PLACE' DOES NOT EXIST).

PUT ASIDE ALL THOUGHTS OF THE RIGHT SPACE (THERE IS NO SUCH THING).

Because:

YOU HAVE NOW 'ARRIVED' AT A 'SPACE' THAT IS... INFINITE... AND MOST IMPORTANTLY... YOURS.

A CALL TO ARMS

YOU are now ready to pursue the form of RESISTANCE that we call

DEBRISM.

BUT WHERE TO BEGIN?

1.

Never finish anything.
This is the first and most important rule of Debrism.[23]

23 (The) Failure (to Fail):

The artist Philip Guston (having been a committed political muralist/Abstract expressionist/Neo-expressionist), pulled off a disastrous magic trick ten years before his death. Perhaps believing he was a mediocrity and deeply dissatisfied, Guston attempted an act of grand Debrism – "Better to be the worst painter in the world than a mediocrity," he thought. And overnight, he made himself so – he re-presented himself, or so he thought, as the greatest enemy of the Cultural Gatekeeper: the bad artist. Hoping – no doubt – that he was finally free (from the Culture Industry) and able live out his remaining years in obscurity, daubing paint on to canvas for his own amusement.

But it was not to be.

Guston walked into a trap. The initial mistake he made was simple: he told his own truth. Your own truth is good – but Guston's great error was in choosing 'authenticating materials' with which to tell it (oil paint, canvas). Guston's second mistake was that he chose an 'authenticating context' (the RIGHT SPACE) in which to unveil to the world his 'new direction'/'bad art'. His intention, perhaps, was to shock the Cultural Gatekeepers to such a degree that he would be ostracized as a culture worker and therefore free to do as he pleased. An elementary error: there is nothing the Cultural Gatekeeper enjoys more than being shocked (providing it is within the correct context and their fellow Cultural Gatekeepers are also present; meaning they are 'collectively shocked' and can immediately agree that this – within the limits of the cultural/political mores of the time – is a good thing). Unwittingly, Guston had sealed his own fate – not least because his 'cartoon-like daubings' were deeply flawed; his natural skill as a draughtsman betraying his Debrist intent – these paintings were compositionally attractive, despite his greatest efforts to make them not so. But most importantly, the artist made the mistake of first exhibiting this 'new direction' at the Marlborough Gallery: a well-known and respected 'authenticating context' located in New York – a city that was, at that time, the very heart of the late 20th century 'art world'.

Guston's grave mistake, in terms of Debrism, could have been easily corrected; had the artist's mind not been so firmly entrenched in completion and authentication. If Guston had truly wanted to free himself from accolades/success/the Culture Industry, he would simply have failed to produce any paintings at all – he would've sat in his studio, staring at a blank canvas throughout the remaining years of his life.

However, as Guston was, it seems, unwilling to take such a purist Debrist position – suffering perhaps from the 'need to create' – there were still other options open to him once his paintings were complete:

A. He could have unveiled his 'new direction' at a local (rural, Upstate New York) arts cafe, turned up morbidly drunk to the opening, sat in a corner and accidentally soiled himself.

Or more effectively:

B. He might have committed this 'new direction' exclusively to the back pages of a local (rural, Upstate New York) newspaper (the painted canvases being disposed of once they had been photographed for purposes of reproduction – the film/photographic images of the canvases being destroyed once the newspaper had been printed).

Or he may even have:

C. Chosen to embrace – perhaps even pioneered – the 'straight to tote bag' format (in a bold leap: completely bypassing the standard 'museum collection reprinted on to tote bag memento available only from the museum store' axis. Then, as above, the paintings/photographs of the paintings are destroyed, once the tote bags have been produced: this manoeuvre being not dissimilar – pre-Netflix – to how a 'bad movie' went 'direct to DVD' – i.e. to a non-authenticating context).

It is just this kind of simple flaw, not fully considering either the medium on to which – or – the context within which one's work is presented (if at all), that invalidates most would-be acts of Debrism.

Consequently, in the final years of his life, Guston became a 'success' to such a degree that his cartoon-like self-portraits (of the lonely artist painting under a single exposed lightbulb, while wearing a Ku Klux Klan hood) passed into the stuff of legend, brought millions of dollars at auction and – most cruelly of all – were made into enormously popular postcards and distributed through Cultural Gatekeeper-owned museum stores all over the world: affordable mementoes, reminding even 'the general public' of the artist's failure to free himself from the Culture Industry.*

* This is a situation that has only recently (2020/21) 'corrected itself' – when, over 40 years after Guston's death – either the 'cancel culture' phenomena – or an authentic concern about the imagery used in Guston's paintings – has seen the seemingly indefinite 'postponement' of a major (travelling) museum retrospective of the artist's work.

In a joint statement, the museum directors (of the National Gallery of Art, Washington; Museum of Fine Arts, Houston; Tate Modern, London; Museum of Fine Arts, Boston) said that they were, "postponing the [Guston] exhibition until a time at which we think† that the powerful message of social and racial justice that is at the center of Philip Guston's work can be more clearly interpreted."

†

Text by Scott King
Design by Scott King and Richard Massey
Additional design by Rhys Atkinson
Printed by Taylor Brothers Bristol Ltd

ISBN 978-1-5272-9386-1

ACT 1 | 'The Debrist Manifesto'
Published by International General, 2021